EDGE BOOKS™

Robots

HOW Robots WORK

BY JENNY MOSS

CAPSTONE PRESS
a capstone imprint

Edge Books are published by Capstone Press,
1710 Roe Crest Drive, North Mankato, Minnesota 56003
www.capstonepub.com

Copyright © 2013 by Capstone Press, a Capstone imprint. All rights reserved.
No part of this publication may be reproduced in whole or in part, or stored in a
retrieval system, or transmitted in any form or by any means, electronic, mechanical,
photocopying, recording, or otherwise, without written permission of the publisher.

Library of Congress Cataloging-in-Publication Data
Moss, Jenny, 1958–
  How robots work / by Jenny Moss.
     p. cm.—(Edge books. Robots)
  Includes bibliographical references and index.
  Summary: "Explains how and where robots work today, as well as discusses new
and developing advances in robotics"—Provided by publisher.
  ISBN 978-1-4296-9919-8 (library binding)
  ISBN 978-1-62065-780-5 (paperback)
  ISBN 978-1-4765-1558-8 (ebook PDF)
1. Robots—Juvenile literature. 2. Robotics—Juvenile literature. I. Title.
  TJ211.2.M685 2013
  629.8'92—dc23   2012026441

Editorial Credits
Christopher L. Harbo, editor; Ted Williams, designer; Eric Gohl, media researcher;
Laura Manthe, production specialist

Photo Credits
AP Images: Seth Wenig, 25; Courtesy of Rotundus: 21; DVIC: Cherie Cullen, 6
(bottom); Getty Images: AFP/Toshifumi Kitamura, 11, Bloomberg/Tony Avelar, 5,
26, Library of Congress, 6 (top); iStockphotos: Torsten Stahlberg, 22–23; NASA: 18,
29; RoboGames: Alan Musselman, 15, Dave Schumaker, 12; Super Stock Inc.: age
fotostock/Javier Larrea, 9, Belinda Images, cover, Prisma, 17

Design Elements: Shutterstock

Capstone Press thanks professor Nicola J. Ferrier from the Department of Mechanical
Engineering at the University of Wisconsin-Madison for her help with this book.

Printed in the United States of America in Stevens Point, Wisconsin.
092012   006937WZS13

Table of
CONTENTS

The World of Robotics

Meet HERB. It has wheels for legs, no face, and must "think" hard to pick up a juice bottle. What is HERB? It's a Home Exploring Robotic Butler. Someday HERB could help do household chores. But right now HERB takes a long time to do one thing. To figure out why, let's learn more about robots.

Robots come in many shapes and sizes, and they have many different abilities. A robot can look like a small insect, a rolling ball, a headless dog, or even a human. But no matter what a robot looks like, its purpose is to help us out. Robots often do jobs that are very difficult or dangerous for people to do. They also do repetitive jobs that would be dull for people.

ROBOT FACT

HERB was built at the Personal Robotics Lab at Carnegie Mellon University in Pittsburgh, Pennsylvania. The lab's goal is to develop robots that can help people in their homes.

A research engineer makes an adjustment to HERB as the robot tries to pick up a juice bottle.

Unimate robots help build cars on an
assembly line at an auto plant in 1970.

Warrior and PackBot

In 2011 an earthquake and tsunami
damaged a nuclear power plant in Japan.
Radiation leaks posed serious health risks to
anyone entering the plant. To help clean up,
a U.S. company sent several Warrior and
PackBot robots to the scene. These small, mobile
robots have tracks that helped them roll over
rough terrain and debris. They also have video
cameras that allowed workers to see the disaster
scene without ever getting near it.

Robotics History

Some robots seem like machines of the future, but robots have a long past. The first use of the word "robot" was in a 1921 play by Karel Capek. The word comes from the Czech word for "worker." Twenty years later, science fiction writer Isaac Asimov used the word "robotics." It means the study, design, and building of robots. In the 1950s, Asimov's writings inspired inventor George Devol and engineer Joseph Engelberger. They designed and built Unimate, the first modern industrial robot. Many Unimate robots soon worked in car factories.

Today robots are everywhere. They package bread, ice cream, candy, and chips. They disarm bombs for the police. In Japan robots chop vegetables and make sushi. Robots sometimes make their jobs look easy. But the science behind the machines can be very complex.

ROBOT FACT

People have been dreaming about humanlike machines for hundreds of years. In the 1400s, Italian artist and inventor Leonardo da Vinci drew plans for robot knights.

How Does a Robot Do That?

Many robots look simple. Their basic shapes and careful movements make them seem easy to design. After all, we can pick up a piece of chocolate and put it in a box. Why can't a robot? But people have brains, legs, arms, eyes, ears, fingers, and noses. For robots to do things people can do, they must have senses and features similar to people.

The Brain

A robot's brain is its computer. The **central processing unit** (CPU) is a major part of the computer. It controls the robot by sending commands to its moving parts. These commands are defined by a software program. This set of instructions tells the robot what to do.

central processing unit—the part of a computer that carries out the instructions of a computer program

An engineer programs a robotic arm with the instructions it needs to do its job at a factory.

A robot can only do what it is programmed to do. The real brains behind robots are roboticists. These people design, build, and program robots. A roboticist can make a robot do new tasks by rewriting its computer software.

The Muscles

A robot needs moving parts to do its tasks. Mechanical devices called **actuators** make movement happen. Actuators are a little like the muscles moving our arms and legs. But they often look like cylinders, boxes, or long rectangles. Their shape depends on what they need to do.

Like our muscles, actuators need energy to work. Actuators use electricity, air pressure, or fluid pressure for power. Most robotic actuators use quiet electric motors.

actuator—a mechanical device for moving or controlling something

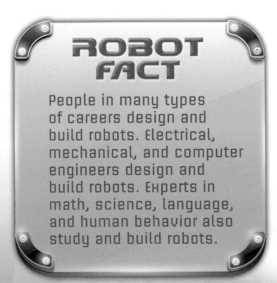

ROBOT FACT

People in many types of careers design and build robots. Electrical, mechanical, and computer engineers design and build robots. Experts in math, science, language, and human behavior also study and build robots.

actuators

Large actuators on a Japanese rescue robot help it pick up heavy debris at the scene of a staged car accident.

A robotic arm with a clawlike gripper
plays chess against human competitors.

The Limbs

Most robots are on the move. They either
travel or busily work on things in front of them.
A traveling robot may have wheels, tracks, legs, or
even propellers—all set in motion by actuators.

To do special tasks, robots are fitted with end effectors. These tools may include saws, spray painters, blowtorches, drills, or grippers. A gripper usually has a thumb and one or more fingers. It can grasp small objects like bolts and screws. Magnetic grippers can lift flat sheets of metal. Vacuum grippers can pick up windshields in auto factories.

end effector—a tool attached to the end of a robotic arm

ROBOT FACT

The European HANDLE project is focused on designing a robotic hand. It moves and senses like a human hand does. It can pick up soft or fragile objects without squishing or breaking them.

The Senses

A robot can't do its job without its sensors. These small devices are the eyes, ears, nose, and sense of touch for the robot. Sensors collect **data** about the robot and its surroundings. This information tells the computer what's going on so it can control the robot's behavior.

All sorts of sensors help out robots. Cameras allow robots to see and follow moving objects. Motion sensors on wheels measure speed. Pressure sensors in robotic hands let the computer know if it's squeezing something too tight. **Infrared** and **ultrasound** sensors detect objects in a robot's path. They send out beams of light or sound signals that bounce off objects and return to the sensor. Smell sensors detect dangerous chemicals or gas leaks. Microphones find the direction of sounds. All of these sensors give robots the information they need to do their work.

data—information or facts

infrared—relating to light waves in the electromagnetic spectrum between visible light and microwaves

ultrasound—relating to sound that is too high for humans to hear

ROBOT FACT

Some robots need senses that humans don't have. A robot might need sensors to detect radiation levels or be able to see in the dark.

camera

The camera on this robot helps it track objects moving in front of it.

Types of Robots

While robots have similar parts, not all are created equal. Robots built to do one task have simpler designs. Robots built to do many things have more complex designs.

Robotic Arms

The robotic arm is the most common type of robot. More than 1 million robotic arms work in factories all over the world. The arm does the same task the exact same way countless times a day. Robotic arms are good for making products such as cars, CDs, and electronic devices because their repetitive work needs to be exact.

ROBOT FACT

Robotic arms are used to twist caps onto peanut butter jars and to test baseball bats.

Sparks fly as robotic arms work together to assemble a car in a factory.

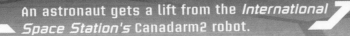
Robotic Arms in Space

One robotic arm that wasn't shut away in a factory was NASA's remote manipulator system (RMS). Space shuttle crews used the 50-foot- (15.2-meter-) long RMS to lift satellites out of the shuttle's cargo area. Astronauts also used it to check the outside of the shuttle for damage. Although space shuttles no longer fly, robotic arms like the RMS help build and fix the *International Space Station.* This large laboratory in space provides a place for scientists and astronauts to conduct research.

A robotic arm is usually mounted on the floor, ceiling, wall, or a metal frame. It is divided into several parts that are connected by rotating joints. Most robotic arms have seven segments connected by six joints. These segments and joints give the arm six **degrees of freedom**. An arm's degrees of freedom control the number of ways it can move, such as up and down, left to right, and front to back.

Most robotic arms are industrial robots for the electronics and automotive industries. These arms work side by side on assembly lines, hovering over conveyor belts. They put together cell phones and other products piece by piece.

 degree of freedom—any of a limited number of ways something can move

ROBOT FACT

Robot arms can even be found in some hospital operating rooms. The da Vinci Surgical System helps surgeons perform difficult heart surgeries.

Mobile Robots

Not all jobs can be done with a robot fixed in one place. Mobile robots explore dangerous volcanoes, collapsing buildings, and even the planet Mars.

A mobile robot gets from place to place using tracks, wheels, or legs. A robot with wheels is simpler to design and can move quickly. GroundBot is a round rolling robot. It quietly travels up to 6 miles (10 kilometers) per hour through rain, snow, mud, and sand. Airports can use these robots to keep an eye on people acting suspiciously.

Wheeled robots sometimes have trouble getting past objects in their paths. A walking robot is more flexible, but it is also trickier to build. Its legs are divided into segments that must work together. However, the more legs the robot has, the more stable it becomes. Some walking robots look like scurrying insects.

Two cameras allow GroundBot's operator to see in any direction as the robot rolls around an airport.

The Roomba's sensors allow the robot to avoid and vacuum around objects such as table legs.

Autonomous Robots

Some robots are controlled by people. A person drives the robot by watching pictures and data on a monitor. But an **autonomous** robot, like the flat, circular Roomba vacuum cleaner, moves on its own using sensor-gathered data.

More than 7 million Roombas currently clean floors in homes around the world. They scoot around and under desks and chairs. They twirl in another direction when they bump into walls. Sensors let them know when all the dirt is gone.

autonomous—able to control oneself; autonomous robots are not operated remotely by a person

Robots of the Future

In 1956 computer scientist John McCarthy was the first to use the phrase "artificial intelligence" (AI). It described the ability of computers and robots to think like people. Today roboticists are developing robots that reason, plan, and learn like people do.

While we're a long way from creating robots that think, AI advancements have been made. In 1997 the IBM supercomputer Deep Blue defeated a chess champion. In 2011 IBM's supercomputer named Watson played *Jeopardy!* against people and won.

artificial intelligence—**the ability of a machine to think like a person**

supercomputer—**a very powerful computer system**

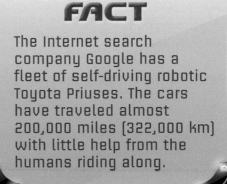

ROBOT FACT

The Internet search company Google has a fleet of self-driving robotic Toyota Priuses. The cars have traveled almost 200,000 miles (322,000 km) with little help from the humans riding along.

IBM's supercomputer Watson takes an early lead over past show champion, Ken Jennings, in a *Jeopardy!* match.

HERB's robotic hand prepares to grab and lift a juice bottle.

Back to HERB

Remember HERB, the butler robot? Why does it take so long for HERB to grab a juice bottle? After all, a robotic arm can be programmed to do a certain task, like pick up a bag. But scientists want HERB to figure things out on its own. They have developed ways for HERB to "think" by using a spinning laser beam to create a 3-D map. Then HERB uses the map to look through a group of pictures to find one that matches a specific object, such as a juice bottle. Success!

ROBOT FACT

Picking up juice bottles isn't the only task HERB can do. The robot can also follow simple instructions to heat up a frozen meal in a microwave.

Cool robots are popping up all over the world and beyond. In 2011 Robonaut 2 arrived at the *International Space Station*. Its mission is to help astronauts with dangerous and repetitive tasks. On February 15, 2012, Robonaut 2 shook hands with station commander Dan Burbank. It was the first handshake between a person and a robot in space. It will be exciting to see where robots go and what they do next!

ROBOT FACT

To make a robot look more human, some roboticists cover the robot's metal skull with frubber. This plastic substance is very stretchy. It gives the robot more real-looking skin.

Robot Swarms

Scientists want to find ways for a swarm of robots to talk to one another and work together. At Harvard University, tiny insectlike Kilobots are being studied. Individually, these quarter-sized, three-legged robots are cheap and easy to build. But they can be programmed to work together like ants to communicate, sense distances, and follow each other around. One day robot swarms may build structures together.

Astronaut Dan Burbank shakes hands with Robonaut 2 on the *International Space Station.*

Glossary

actuator (AK-choo-ay-tur)—a mechanical device for moving or controlling something

artificial intelligence (ar-ti-FISH-uhl in-TEL-uh-junss)—the ability of a machine to think like a person

autonomous (aw-TAH-nuh-muhss)—able to control oneself; autonomous robots are not operated remotely by a person

central processing unit (SEN-truhl PROS-ess-ing YOO-nit)—the part of a computer that carries out the instructions of a computer program

data (DAY-tuh)—information or facts

degree of freedom (di-GREE UV FREE-duhm)—any of a limited number of ways something can move

end effector (END uh-FEKT-ur)—a tool attached to the end of a robotic arm

infrared (in-fruh-RED)—relating to light waves in the electromagnetic spectrum between visible light and microwaves

radiation (ray-dee-AY-shuhn)—tiny particles sent out from radioactive material; radiation is dangerous to people

supercomputer (SOO-pur-kuhm-pyoo-tur)—a very powerful computer system

ultrasound (UHL-truh-sound)—relating to sound that is too high for humans to hear

Read More

Brasch, Nicolas. *Robots and Artificial Intelligence.* The Technology Behind. Mankato, Minn.: Smart Apple Media, 2011.

Chaffee, Joel. *How to Build a Prize-Winning Robot.* Robotics. New York: Rosen Pub.'s Central Rosen, 2011.

Davis, Barbara J. *The Kids' Guide to Robots.* Kids' Guides. Mankato, Minn.: Capstone Press, 2010.

Payment, Simone. *Robotics Careers: Preparing for the Future.* Robotics. New York: Rosen Central, 2011.

Internet Sites

FactHound offers a safe, fun way to find Internet sites related to this book. All of the sites on FactHound have been researched by our staff.

Here's all you do:

Visit *www.facthound.com*

Type in this code: 9781429699198

Check out projects, games and lots more at
www.capstonekids.com

Index

actuators, 10, 11, 12
artificial intelligence, 24
Asimov, Isaac, 7
autonomous robots,
    22–23

Canadarm2, 18
Capek, Karel, 7
central processing units
    (CPUs), 8

da Vinci, Leonardo, 7
Deep Blue, 24
degrees of freedom, 19
Devol, George, 7

end effectors, 13
Engelberger, Joseph, 7

frubber, 28

GroundBots, 20, 21

Home Exploring Robotic
    Butler (HERB), 4, 5,
    26, 27

Kilobots, 28

mobile robots, 6, 20, 21

PackBots, 6

remote manipulator
    system (RMS), 18
Robonaut 2, 28, 29
robot cars, 24
robotic arms, 9, 12, 16–19
robotic hands, 13
roboticists, 9, 24, 28
robot swarms, 28
Roombas, 22–23

sensors, 14, 15, 22, 23
software, 8, 9
supercomputers, 24

Unimates, 6, 7

Warriors, 6
Watson, 24, 25